PERFECTION LEARNING®

The
Tools of Science

Cathy Elliott

Table of Contents

The Scientific Method

1

Have you ever asked questions about why or how something happens? Scientists wonder about things too. They use the **scientific method** to find answers to their questions.

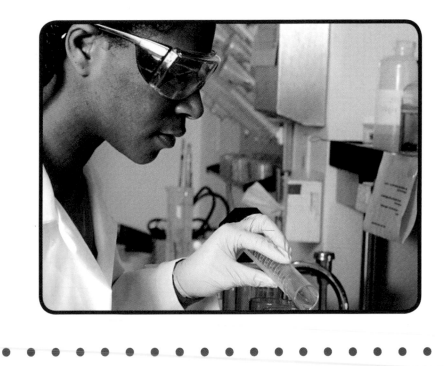

The first step in the scientific method is stating the **problem** or the question. Once a scientist has a question, she finds out all she can about the topic. Then she forms a **hypothesis**, or guess, about the answer to the question.

Next, the scientist does an **experiment** to see if her guess is correct.

A scientist often does the same experiment over and over. If the result is always the same, the hypothesis becomes a **theory**. A theory is something that is probably true.

You can use the scientific method to do an experiment. The tools of science will help you.

Steps in the Scientific Method

1. Choose a problem.

2. Make **observations** to learn about the problem.

3. Form a hypothesis.

4. Experiment to test the hypothesis.

5. Decide what the results of the experiment say about the problem.

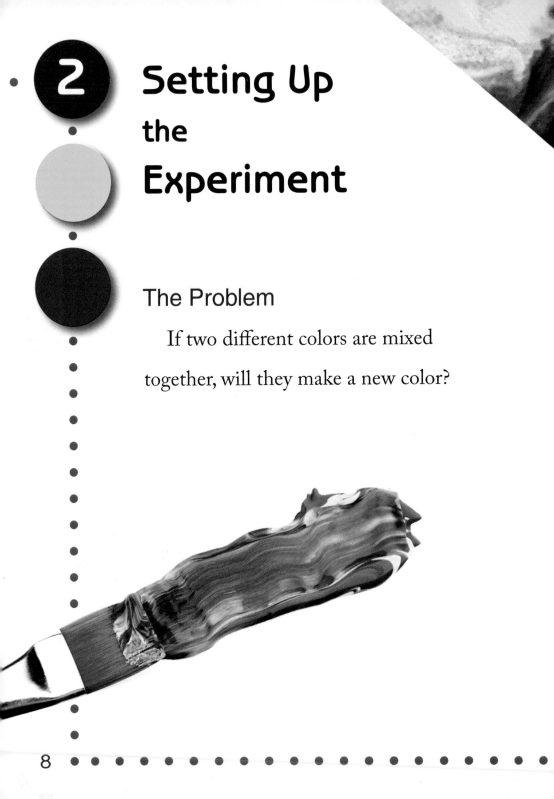

2 Setting Up the Experiment

The Problem

If two different colors are mixed together, will they make a new color?